The Life and Times of

Thomas Hiram Holding (1884 – 1930)

Compiled and written by Carl White

Table of Contents

Title page	4
Family Members	5
Quotations	6
Family Tree	7/8
Notes	9
Foreword	10
The Mormon Route West - Map	11/12
Thomas Hiram Holding – The Boy	15
Thomas Hiram Holding – The Man	49
Afterword	66
Acknowledgements	70
Contacts	71

Thomas Hiram Holding's family

His parents –

Daniel and Sarah Holding (nee Middleton)

Their children -

Thomas Hiram Holding (married Sarah Darlington)

Daniel Holding (died young)

Sarah Jane Holding (married James Johnstone Bryden)

Ephraim George Holding (married Mary Jane Clifton)

Margaret Hannah Holding (died young)

Josephine Holding (died young)

Joseph Holding (died young)

Richard Holding (married Rose Hannah 'Rosanna' Smith)

Mary Ann Holding (married Bedson Eardley)

Thomas Clayton Holding (first wife Lovina Clayton Pollard, second wife Catherine Davis).

Maria Clayton Holding (died young).

Quotations

From England –

We live in deeds, not years;   in thoughts, not breaths,

in feelings,   not in figures on a dial.

English poet – Philip James Bailey (1816 – 1902).

From the United States of America -

Life is the only art that we are required to practice without preparation, and without being allowed the preliminary trials, the failures and the botches, that are essential for training.

American Historian, Lewis Mumford (1895 – 1990).

Holding Ancestry 1568 to 1720

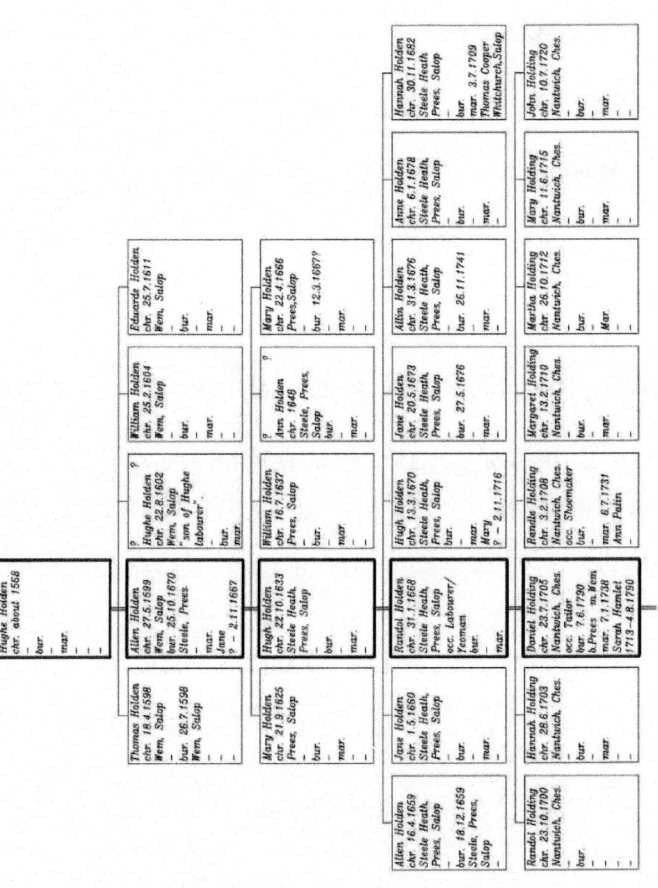

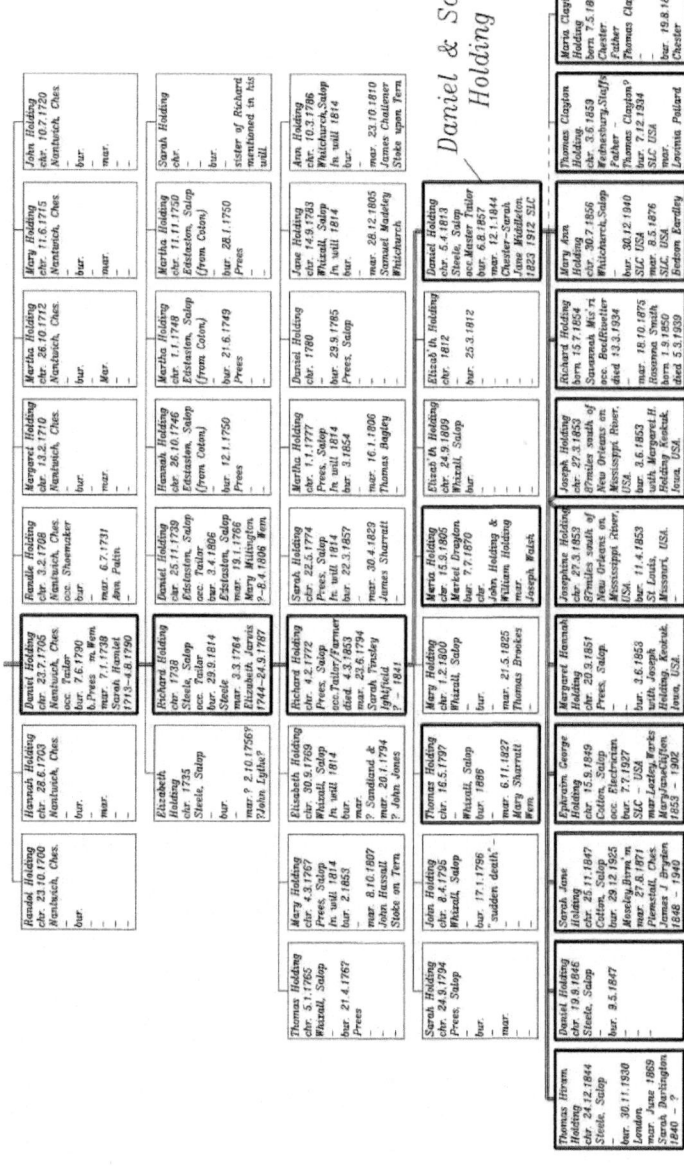

Holding Ancestry 1700 to 1900

Notes

Whilst much of the research for this book is original and subject to copyright laws, there is plenty that has been compiled from information received from a variety of sources over the past three decades or so. Unfortunately the names of these contributors have been lost in the mists of time. It is hoped that the publication of this work will not cause offence, but if that is the case, then the writer will be pleased to make corrections in future editions.

Quotations that are generally italicised, are reproduced exactly as the original document, complete with lack of punctuation, grammatical, spelling errors, etc. To note these errors in customary fashion – sic – would be too tedious and for this reason the writer has refrained from doing so.

Foreword

It is quite hard to grasp the fact that less than two hundred years ago the interior of North America was, to a large extent, an unexplored wilderness. Before that, the region between the Mississippi River and the Rocky Mountains was largely the domain of indigenous tribes and the occasional French fur trapper. In southern regions, the Santa Fe Trail was used by mule trains to fringe the Rockies, but the discovery of a route suitable for horse-drawn wagons had to wait until the arrival of the nineteenth century. In short, North America was split into two coastal regions and if you wanted to travel from the east to California in the west, then there was little choice other than to sail around the southern tip of South America, which to put it mildly, was not without its hazards.

The key to unlocking the interior came with the Louisiana Purchase in 1803, when the United States, as it was then, purchased 900,000 square miles from Napoleon who needed the cash to fund his wars in Europe. America was not slow off the mark and the following year their president Thomas Jefferson despatched Captain Meriwether Lewis and Lieutenant William Clark on horseback to, amongst other things, find a suitable route through the Rockies to permit the passage of horse-drawn wagons. In that regard they were unsuccessful and the discovery of the only crossing point on the Continental Divide, South Pass, came in 1812 when Scottish fur trader Robert Stuart stumbled across it. The first attempt to take wagons over had to wait a further two decades until in 1832 when Captain Benjamin Bonneville led a caravan of 20 wagons. That act opened the flood gates and soon the prairies and mountains were alive with trains of 'prairie schooners' heading west. Over the next 40 years or so 400,000 souls would take on the challenge and at least 20,000 of them would perish along the way. Three of these were the siblings of Thomas Hiram Holding.

Nothing illustrates the scale of that exodus more than Deep Rut Hill in Wyoming where the wheels of almost 100,000 wagons have cut their way through solid rock.

Deep Rut Hill, Wyoming

Amongst the early pioneers were farmers seeking to stake a claim to rich arable farmland, gold prospectors and a minority religious sect attempting to escape persecution.

The Mormon religion was founded in upstate New York by Joseph Smith, who in 1823 discovered a box containing several engraved gold plates. Persecution gradually pushed Smith and his followers further west and this culminated in his, and his brother Hirum's, assassination in Carthage, Illinois in 1844. Three years later their new leader Brigham Young followed in Benjamin Bonneville's footsteps and led a small group of wagons across the plains and over the Rockies at South Pass. As Young descended into the Great Salt Lake Basin he declared, 'This is the Place' and there he laid the foundations of Salt Lake City.

Mormon missionaries had been active in Europe from as early as 1837, but now the process was accelerated to bring in skilled labour to help build their new city. This forms the rapidly developing tapestry into which the family of Thomas Hiram Holding became immersed.

Thomas Hiram's mother Sarah Middleton was baptised into the Mormon religion at some time before 1841 whilst her future husband Daniel Holding was baptised in 1843. They were married in January of the following year, with their first child Thomas Hiram Holding being baptised in December 1844. The Christian name Hiram may have been taken in honour of Joseph Smith's elder brother, Hyrum Smith, who had been assassinated earlier in that same year. As the family made plans to travel to the Great Salt Lake, it remains very doubtful if they ever fully realised the full extent of the trials and tribulations that that decision would bring to them. Their quiet rural upbringing would never have prepared them for the challenges that lay ahead. Whilst these challenges would be the making of Thomas Hiram, they may well have been the breaking of his father Daniel. However, as we shall see their mother Sarah was made of sterner stuff.

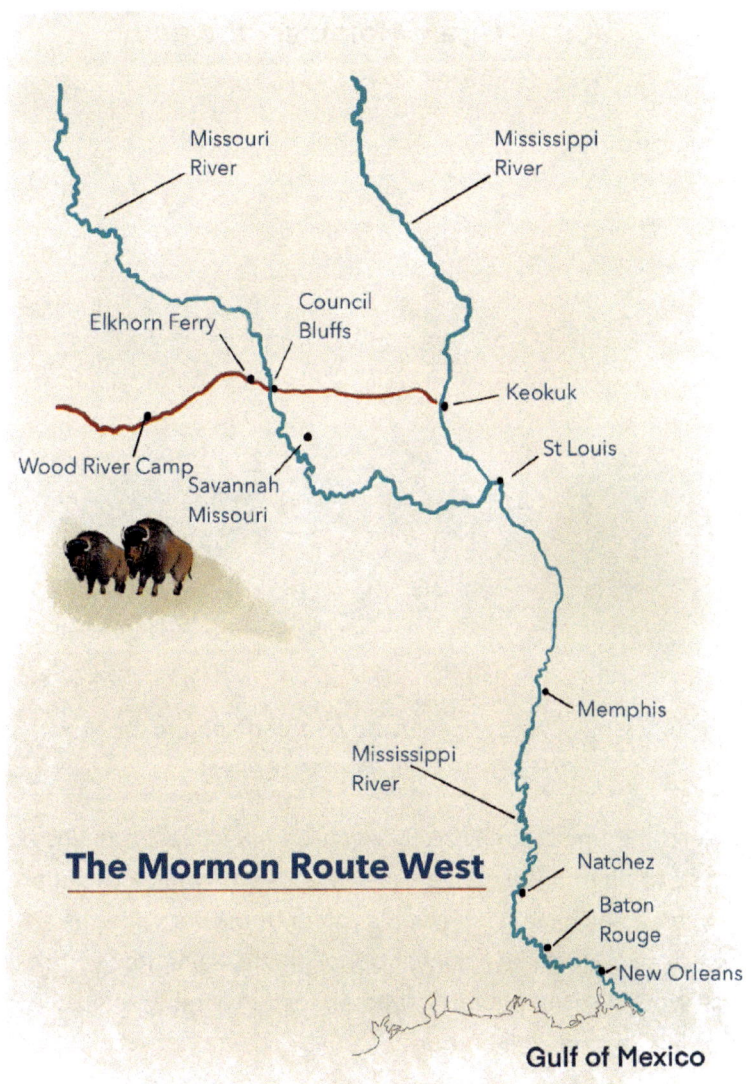

Thomas Hiram Holding – the boy

The 'Jersey' sailing ship leaving Liverpool, bound for New Orleans, 1853 by Frederick Piercy.

Researching one's family history can be addictive. It might be likened to an infinitely large jigsaw puzzle, for which, if you are lucky, you may have been given a rough framework and the odd piece or two. Just like a conventional puzzle, each time you fit a piece you receive a 'buzz' that almost inevitably sends you scurrying off in search of more.

It was my wife's Aunt Kath who gave us our first 'fix' when, some forty years or so ago, she handed us a type-written, grubby sheet of paper. This described how in the 1850s, my wife's great-great-paternal grandparents, Daniel and Sarah Holding, trekked across North America with the Latter Day Saints, in search of their Zion in the West. In my younger years,

I loved reading and watching cowboy epics and I was immediately hooked. I wanted to know more, but work and family commitments meant that the grubby sheet of paper was, for the time being at least, put on the back burner.

Many years later, once the children had gone their own ways, I resurrected the story and I pondered. The time was now right, the Internet had arrived, and Mormon records were impeccable. For example, these records not only list the names of everyone on the sailing ship and wagon train but also where they camped and the time they moved on the following morning. Not only were we blessed with Mormon records, but also with Frederick Piercy's book, *Route from Liverpool to Great Salt Lake Valley*, first published in 1855.

The purpose of his book is best told in his own words:

> *On the 5th day of February, 1853, in compliance with previous arrangements, I* embarked *on the 'Jersey' for New Orleans, on my way to the Great Salt Lake Valley. My object was to make sketches of the most principal and interesting places along the Route.*

By a fortunate coincidence, the *Jersey* left Liverpool just ten days before Daniel and Sarah Holding on board the sailing ship *Elvira Owen*. As Frederick took time out to sketch, it was inevitable that their paths would have crossed, and the scenes that he illustrated would have been much the same as the Holding family's experience. Many of his evocative sketches have been used to illustrate this book.

However, our good fortune as family history researchers does not end there. Some 75 years after the family emigrated, Daniel and Sarah's eldest child, Thomas Hiram Holding, wrote a letter that summed up the experience and the intervening years. In this, he movingly described how he had returned to the churchyard in the village of Prees to pay his respects to his father, Daniel, who had been buried there: *'More than once I have tried to find the Mound ie grave but alas theres hundreds buried there and Poor Daniel Holding the tailor cant be found.'*

However, we have jumped ahead of ourselves, we need to start our story with a visit to the small village of Prees in Shropshire, where going back to at least the mid-1500s, generations of the Holding clan had farmed on smallholdings. Intriguingly, in his book *Family Names and their Story*, S. Baring Gould defines the surname as follows: *Holding – 'A Norse hauld was a superior yeoman holding allodial land'.* Note – 'allodial' means much the same as 'freehold'.

By the mid-1800s, it was usual for the head of the family to be authoritarian and in that regard, Thomas Hiram's grandfather, Richard Holding, was no exception. He had, as they say, married well and owned a few modest dwellings, which he had promised to pass on to his descendants. He was well known in the locality, perhaps even well respected, but from this distance in time, it is hard to be certain.

Daniel's birth was recorded on 5 April 1813, the youngest of eight children of Richard and Sarah (nee Tinsley). Daniel and local girl Sarah Jane Middleton were married on 2 January 1844 at the church of St John's in Chester. Sarah Jane, who was ten years younger than Daniel, was the daughter of Abraham and Jane Middleton. At the time of their marriage, at least five members of Sarah Jane's family had converted to Mormonism, whilst Daniel's conversion had taken place in the year before their marriage. The background to his conversion is told in the following extract from his diary, written exactly as he recorded it, without punctuation and complete with spelling errors, but the fact that he could write at all perhaps indicates that he was educated to an above-average standard.

Daniel Holding His Book – June 11 1845 – Prees Wood England.

I came to a knolidge of the truth by preaying to the Lord for knolidge to know which was right and by reeding Every Night a chapter and preaying for the Lord to shoe me the true way I begun at the begining of Mathaw and continaud to reed a chapter Night by Night with a Determation not to leave of till the Lord revealed to me the troue way I continued to reed Night by Night throw St Mathaue and St Mark and St Look Gospell The last Night I read the Last Chapter of St Look Gospell when that Night I had a Gloreas Vision on my Bed I had the End of his present World shoead before me and The Mileniel or Reaighen of Peace all in joing peace and harmoney and I saw the Saviaur in the midst Oh it was gloreaious to behould More than Toang can express or pen rite The gloreais of those peeple I saw sitting under theair one Vine and Fig tree Oh happy Time Whilst on the other hand the Wicked of this present world was truly alfull All fases gethren Blackness Some running tuea and fraue and calling for the rocks and Mountains to fall on them The seen was aful In this situation I was pleased in I heard a Voice se 'Which wilt goe tow of these company?' The voice sead 'if thoue wilt join that happey People thou must join the Later day saints' I must goe to one company or the other I was not long making my choice The Next morning in teaes to think how I had abaused The saints The Next Day I went to the House of Brother Wigin of Cotton went in and sat Down between Brother Wiggin and Autha Smith The look surprised and wondred to see me theair

As I never called no never as I believed them all to be Fouls and rong but a few words from me soon Brother Wiggin sead 'oh you can begin to see a little' and I said 'yes' and in a few days I was Babtized I tould Brother Wiggins I had Better be Babtized in the Night because of My Works I continuad to reed my Bible I red the Words of The Saviaur He that is a sham of Me and my word of him 'shall the son of Man be a shamed?' These words went to my hart I then tould all I saw that I was going to abay the Gospell On a Sunday afternoon I was Babtised in the presence of hundrerds............ March 1843.

I hope these lines will goe to the Land of Sion wether I live or not to be had in Everlasting remembrance. Daniel Holding. Presiding Elder in the Church of Jesus Christ of latter Day Saints. This day July 23. Cotton Wood 1847.

Future events show that the news of Daniel's conversion did not sit comfortably with his father, Richard, or with the parish church of St Chad's, Prees, where the name of Daniel's ancestors is, even today, commemorated throughout the building and churchyard. Despite that, life for Daniel's family over the next few years appears to have continued much as normal when, during that time, Sarah gave birth to five children; the eldest Thomas Hiram (born 1844), Daniel who unfortunately died young, Sarah Jane (born 1847), Ephraim George (born 1849) and Margaret Hannah (born 1851). The family's opportunity to emigrate came during Sarah's sixth pregnancy, when in 1853 they said farewell to their family and friends and set off walking the forty-odd miles to Liverpool. Today, it is hard to grasp the enormity of their separation; the chance of ever seeing their loved ones again was very slight.

Richard's bitterness at losing his son was clear to see and best summed up in the words contained in the letter written by his grandson, Thomas Hiram Holding, some 75 years later: *'When the end ie separation was about to be had, unknown to father he cut his portion save £5 only and said: 'serve him right to go gallivanting about to Horse Ponds with so called Saints'. Every horse pond was soon in use for baptising Mormon converts'.*

Painting depicting a Mormon baptism in a horse pond

The timing of the Mormon sailings was carefully planned to ensure that the emigrants passed through New Orleans before humid summer weather fuelled epidemics of yellow fever and cholera, and through the Rocky Mountains before they became unpassable with winter snow.

Before the *'Jersey'* sailing ship slipped her tow - see previous illustration - Frederick Piercy described the scene as follows: *'We were quickly towed down the Mersey, past the Rock Lighthouse and fort at the mouth, and the wind being fair, the sails were soon unfurled and filled, and we stood out to sea.'*

He went on to describe how: *'So we were hauled out of dock, and soon after, a pedlar and an old woman with a basket of trinkets were found "stowed away" aboard. The little fat Captain, who turned out to be a choleric old fellow, flew at the man, like a Turk," punched his head and blacked his eye, and sent both the man and the woman back by the steam tug which brought us out.'*

Ten days later, on 15 February 1853, the Holding family left Liverpool aboard the *Elvira Owen* and made a particularly rapid crossing, during which the emigrants reported that the sea was so rough that, *'water came in everywhere and the passengers rolled from one side to the other in heaps'*. Sooner than expected, they were anchored off the mouth of the Mississippi Delta where, on 23 March, Sarah Holding gave birth to twins who were immediately baptised Joseph and Josephine. After being cleared for quarantine regulations, the ship was towed upriver to New Orleans, known at that time as, *The Gateway into the Interior*.

Manxman James Quayle recorded in his diary, *'Got to the bar of the Mississippi river on 24th day of March, pulled over the bar by steam boats Conqueror and Mary Kingslands after a passage of 37 days. Left Wed. March 30th arrived at New Orleans on Thursday March 31st.*

The experience came as a shock to all, but their main task was to keep thieves from boarding the ship. One trickster who was prevented from boarding said that he needed to come aboard to speak with Pat Murphy, but when told that there was no such person on board, he replied, 'That is a lie, because I have never known a ship without one!'

Despite the time of year, New Orleans was at that time suffering an epidemic of yellow fever and without delay the family soon boarded the paddle steamer, *James Robb,* which would take them 1,350 miles up the Mississippi River to Keokuk, Iowa.

Early photograph showing the crowded Landing Dock at New Orleans

No doubt, at some point along the way, they would have passed Frederick Piercy as he sketched scenes from the banks.

New Orleans, 1853 by Frederick Piercy

Baton Rouge, 1853 by Frederick Piercy

Natchez under the Hill, 1853 by Frederick Piercy

Memphis, 1853 by Frederick Piercy

St Louis, 1853 by Frederick Piercy

Frederick Piercy's idyllic scenes contrast sharply with the experiences endured by our family, as along the way they, unfortunately suffered the loss of their three youngest children; two-year-old Margaret Hannah and the infant twins, Joseph and Josephine. They were buried in simple graves along the river banks, and their father Daniel built fires on top of the mounds to hide the smell and keep the wolves away.

It is perhaps a blessing that at Keokuk they were left with little time to mourn. At the campsite, on the hilltop, they found themselves fully occupied as they prepared the wagon to accompany them on the final 1,300-mile trek to Salt Lake City.

In April of 1853, The Keokuk Dispatch reported that: *'200 Mormons arrived here on Friday last on board the steamboat Hindoo on their way to Salt Lake, several hundred more are lying at St Louis and two and three ship loads expected daily from New Orleans. Those who arrived have gone into camp above*

the city incorporation. They are all native of England and Wales and left the port of Liverpool on 18th February last for New Orleans, where they arrived safely and in good health having lost but one of their number along the way. The whole train when it is made up is expected to number 2,000 persons. They intend to making Keokuk their starting point. Farmers having stock of cattle fit for yoke will here find a ready market'.

By May the same newspaper added: *'800 Mormons have left and 300 more have arrived at the campground. A total of 3,800 are expected to pass through the port this year. The Mormons have behaved in a most peaceful and courteous manner during their stay here and have won the respect and confidence of the community with their orderly and law abiding behaviour'.*

The Campsite at Keokuk, 1853 by Frederick Piercy

Frederick Piercy visited the campsite at dawn one day and described the scene as follows: *'I sallied out in search of the Camp, which, after climbing a steep bluff on the edge of the river, I found most picturesquely situated on the top of the hill, surrounded by wood, and commanding a view of the country for miles around. The situation was admirably chosen, as there were* (sic) *good drainage and an abundance of wood and water combined. It was just daylight, and the guards had returned to their tents. Upon my entrance all was still in the Camp, no person was to be seen.*

The emigrants from each nation had been wisely placed together, and those who had crossed the sea together were still associated as neighbours in Camp. I heard no complaint of sickness, and was told that the general health was good.

The camp was in excellent order and the emigrants informed me that when the ground was not muddy they would rather live in a tent than in a house. I saw few idlers ... the wagons and the tents which with their white covers, looked extremely picturesque amidst the spring foliage of the country'.

Cyrus H. Wheelock would lead the wagon train that consisted of 52 wagons (one occupied by the Holding family), 400 individuals, 17 horses, 2 mules, 216 oxen, 83 cows, 12 heifer (young cows) and one carriage. Frederick Piercy had this to say about Cyrus H. Wheelock: *'I particularly noticed the generosity of with which C. H. Wheelock volunteered the use of his teams for the public good. They were constantly engaged in transporting the luggage of the emigrants from the river to the Camp, which saved many a poor person's scanty means, and rescued many a poor family from a dilemma, for as yet there were very few oxen in the Camp, and most persons were unwilling to run the risk of their animals being worn out before the commencement of the journey'.*

The first part of their journey took them 300 miles from Keokuk on the Mississippi river to Council Bluffs on the Missouri river. Council Bluffs had by 1853 been abandoned as the starting point of the Mormon Trail due to unreliability of water depth in the Missouri river.

The Missouri River and Council Bluffs, 1853 by Frederick Piercy

The Council Bluff's Ferry, 1853 by Frederick Piercy

The Elkhorn River Ferry, 1853 by Frederick Piercy

It is perhaps preferred that we put aside romantic images of horse-drawn *'prairie schooners'*. Those wagons, mainly populated with prospectors and settlers heading west in search of that elusive nugget or that prized plot of land, were usually confined to the Oregon Trail. Whilst that trail followed the north bank of the Platte River, the Mormons confined themselves to the south bank. The former was designed for speed, a race against time, whereas, by comparison, the Mormon wagons were lumbering juggernauts, powered by four bullocks and heavily laden with essential supplies to sustain them in Salt Lake City throughout the winter months. With no spare carrying capacity, the Mormon settlers would walk the 1,300 miles across rough and often muddy ground. They took with them the essential skills to help build their newly founded city in the West. Daniel was a tailor by trade. All was planned with military precision; up with a bugle call at 5 am, every man to carry a gun, or at least have one to hand, no man to stray more than 100 yards from the camp without permission, assembling for prayers at 8.30 pm and lights out by 9 pm.

Accidents with guns were not uncommon, as Mary Ringo, a pioneer on the Oregon Trail reported, *'And now Oh God comes the saddest record of my life for this day my husband shot himself ... if I had no children how gladly I would lay me down with my dead.'* At the time, she was pregnant with her sixth child. At night, the cattle would be unyoked and corralled, wagons arranged in a circle with wheels interlocked, whilst the settlers slept in tents. The adults were tested daily to their limits of endurance while the children found every waking hour an adventure, and as we shall see, the experience provided the eldest boys, 8-year-old Thomas Hiram and 4-year-old Ephraim George, with a foundation onto which they successfully built their adult lives.

Much of the settlers' time on the trail was spent, fording rivers on rafts, double teaming oxen on steep upgrades and manhandling the wagons down steep declines aided by oxen, pulleys and ropes. Freeing bogged-down wagons was particularly challenging and is well illustrated in the following record made by James Pett who had so far accompanied the Holding family on the early part of the trail, *'One of the crew of the old ship 'Elvira Owen' (the carpenter) fell in with one of our Mormon sisters and came up with the company to St Louis and stayed over there a few days and got married and then came to Keokuk with the intention of crossing the plains with some of the companies and bought a wagon, ox team and outfit complete and started out on the fearful muddy road and Smith (that was his name) was not accustomed to such travelling and driving oxen through mud half a leg deep, so after travelling a few miles, he began to despair as he found out that land travelling was far more unpleasant than it was to walk the decks of an ocean schooner under like conditions, and he became very abusive as nothing suited him, and finally he threw down his ox whip and declared that he would not go another step farther. So after a little parleying with his wife, he took his bundle of his clothes and went back to sea, and his wife hired a young man to drive the team and she came to the Valley, and that was the last of Smith'.*

Particularly along the early part of the trail ground conditions were a constant problem. Not only for the wagons but also for the camping grounds, where sudden downpours could leave their tents waterlogged.

However, despite their trials, there were lighter moments. In 1856 Hannah Cornaby wrote, *'the oxen were wild, and getting them yoked was a most laughable sight I ever witnessed; everybody giving orders, and nobody knowing how to carry them out.'*

Her comments are a reminder that the settlers were not hardened frontiersmen, but drawn from all walks of everyday European life.

Cecilia Adams reported: *'Last night my clothes got out of the wagon and an oxen ate them up.'* Frederick Piercy had this comment: *'My attention was suddenly attracted to the spot where I had left it, when I heard a girl cry out, "O look 'ee there! If there isn't a critter a eaten something;" and sure enough there was, for at that moment I saw the bright red corners of my best silk handkerchief vanish into a cow's throat.'*

In 1853, George Belshaw ruefully suggested that, *'In camp the women ruled',* whilst Helen Carpenter, who emigrated in 1857, kept a detailed diary from which the following is an extract:

'The high winds lately have interfered ... with our dresses, blowing them about and leaving the pedal extremities in an immodest condition ... Aunt, sis and Emily pinned some rocks in the bottom of their skirts never dreaming of the black shins they would carry.' Ezra Meeker noted, *'The younger women were rather shy in accepting the inevitable but finally fell into the procession, and we soon had a community of women wearing bloomers.'*

There were more sober moments too; this from Helen Carpenter again, *'Not until the next morning did we see that the camp fire was on a grave ... but it was not moved, I have mentioned a growing indifference ... It is hoped we will not be permanently changed.*

The Camp at Wood River, 1853 by Frederick Piercy

For the most part, and perhaps contrary to popular belief, the Native Americans only wanted to trade. They brought fish and vegetables to swap for clothes and trinkets, but as Ephraim reported, they would also try to sneak up on the wagons to steal clothing. Not only clothing, in later life he remembered that one day they snatched up Ephraim himself, '*they turned and said, "Whoopie Gee!" and all the children screamed and cried, so Daniel conceded and let them have the watch and got his little boy back*'. Sadly, his gold pocket watch had been a treasured gift from his father, Richard.

Chimney Rock, 1853 by Frederick Piercy

Chimney Rock marked the end of the flat prairie land and the start of hilly countryside, which would steadily lead them to the Rocky Mountains and the Continental Divide.

Scott's Bluff, 1853 by Frederick Piercy

"Today we killed a beef for supper, or should I say tried to. Pa and the boys shot at it about 50 times before they got it. Yes, those Indians had better think twice before attacking this dangerous group" – Maria Shrode, 1850.

"Every emigrant seemed to signalise himself by killing a buffalo" – Isaac Foster, 1859.

Fort Laramie, 1853 by Frederick Piercy

Independence Rock, 1853 by Frederick Piercy

Independence Rock was so called because it was said that you needed to reach this point before the 4 July if you were to make it safely through the Rockies before the first snowfall.

Devil's Gate, 1853 by Frederick Piercy

Tragedy struck the Holding family yet again on 29 August, best told in Ephraim's own words again recalled later in his life: *'I am firmly convinced that it was nothing but the direct intervention of Providence that saved my sister's life. My sister* (Sarah Jane) *was six years of age. I was four, and I barely remember the old oxen and the wagon with the place where the incident occurred. We were coming across the plains in Cyrus H. Wheelock's company, and the wagon on which we rode was loaded with freight. In fact the freight completely filled the wagon box to the top or a little above it. My sister and I were playing on top of this wagon when a wheel went into a chuck hole and she was thrown off directly under the wagon. The driver did not notice it and the wagon went on, both the front and rear wheels of this monster freight wagon passing over my poor sister's head'.*

'The people in the wagon train were all of the Church. They did what no other people, I think, would have done out in the plain, alone and far away from medical aid. They gathered up the little girl found her head crushed to pulp with portions of the brain showing. And then all the elders of the wagon train gathered around and submitted their case to a God in whom they devoutly believed and trusted. They prayed for the little girl, then with their hands, anointed her, washed her head as best they could, shoving its skull bones back into shape. Instead of the death that all regarded as certain, the little one lived, and in a very few weeks was playing as usual with me on the wagon top, only more careful to keep away from the edges'.

Sarah Jane's scars remained noticeable for the rest of her life and she lived to celebrate her 78th birthday in 1925.

Witches Rocks, 1853 by Frederick Piercy

The trek proved to be a gruelling test of endurance, as Esther Belle McMillan Hannah reported in 1852, *'Our way seems endless ... Feel very unwell today. Am almost worn down with the fatigue of the constant travel'.* Whilst in that same year, Abigail Jane Stott reported, *'Made twenty miles, we passed eight fresh graves'*.

An early photograph of Mormon wagons passing through Echo Valley in 1853

However, the road was not endless and eventually, the bedraggled train of wagons descended down the long, steep escarpment into The Great Basin and Salt Lake City.

At an average speed of just over 30 miles per day, the 8,000-mile journey from Prees had taken the family eight months. They no doubt received a spirited welcome and their wagons were soon emptied and converted into accommodation to serve as their homes during the coming winter months.

The Great Salt Lake City, 1853 by Frederick Piercy

Before we leave Frederick Piercy and the trail behind, it is worth taking note of the woodcut sketch below, once again created in 1853 by Frederick Piercy.

Approaching Fort Laramie, woodcut by Frederick Piercy

Would it be too fanciful to think that this might be our Holding family as they approached Fort Laramie? Daniel, with whip in hand guiding his wagon, Sarah holding the hands of her two youngest children, Sarah Jane, 6 and Ephraim George, 4 and, we know that they took with them their dog, 'Yuno'. Surely few families would have taken their pet dog with them. If this is the Holding family then we would have to wonder why the subject of this book Thomas Hiram Holding is not shown in the scene. Possibly he was helping on another wagon or even peering over Piercy's shoulder as he sketched the scene. Almost certainly we will never know for certain.

Almost before the family had time to settle into their new life, Daniel appeared to have had doubts. He had lost three children along the way and maybe he questioned if his decision to emigrate had been a wise one. Perhaps he was challenged by the morality of bigamous relationships, openly practised within the city. The final straw, which may have contributed to his decision to return home to Prees, may have come in the form of a letter from home, a letter which had trailed in their wake as they journeyed westwards. This letter, from his elder brother, Thomas, informed him that their father Richard had passed away, just three weeks after their departure from Prees, and the timing of his death, coupled with the fact that Richard had resentfully left Daniel just £5 from his estate, might lead us to conclude that Daniel's departure had possibly hastened his father's demise. His mind was soon made up and as soon as the snow cleared from the South Pass in the Rockies, he would take his family back to Shropshire. There are recorded instances of quitters being stoned by settlers, but wagons had to be returned to Keokuk to serve the next influx of immigrants and it seems likely that Daniel and Sarah made use of themselves in this way. The going would have been much easier now that the wagons were empty and they could ride rather than walk. That said Sarah was now expecting their eighth child, who would be named Richard, in honour of Daniel's deceased father. The birth was said to have taken place on 15 July 1854, in a barn in Savannah, Missouri. His birthplace in Missouri is an indication that the family were following the Missouri River, probably on foot, towards the Mississippi and New Orleans.

It is clear from the foregoing that, 'crossing the plains' was no simple matter; it could make you, break you, or, as evidenced by countless graves that litter the trail, it could even be the end of you. Future events will show that at this time Daniel may have been suffering from a peptic ulcer, perhaps brought on by the trials and tribulations of their epic journey. A peptic ulcer is known to affect one's mood and may account for why Thomas Hiram Holding in later life referred to his father as being, *'a much respected man of fiery temper soon over'*. Whilst Daniel may have harboured doubts, his wife Sarah never lost her faith and in later life she would return to Salt Lake City with three of her children. If their relationship was not being tested, then at the very least there appears to be plenty of scope for disharmony. We cannot be certain of any of this of course, but one thing that we can be certain of is that Sarah now had a newly born child to nurture and thus, more and more responsibility would have fallen onto the shoulders of 9 year old Thomas Hiram Holding. He was now blessed with survival skills aplenty, learned during those most precious formative years, and future events would prove that he revelled in the challenges and adventures of the outdoor life. Daniel no doubt welcomed his eldest son's ability to shoulder more and more of the family's responsibilities.

Around the end of October, Daniel received another letter from his brother Thomas.

QuinaBrook   *September 2nd, 1854*

My Dear Brother,

I hope that this will find you well as it leaves me at present. I received your letter on the 29th of August. I was glad to hear you were all well when it left and very happy to hear that you were got so far back on your road to old England. I hope that your health will, permit you to travel on till you arrive safe back here.

William Holding as left this part of the country and gone to reside in Macklesfield where he as married a Silk Weaver 40 years of age. He sold all Father's Furniture later end of last year and left the place and went to lodge with Williams the Blacksmiths. He was travelling about the country when he met with his wife. Geo. Groom is married and lives in a house under Mr Bowen and his doing the great part of the work you used to have, but know doubt when you come you will have it back as many off your old customers want you back badly.

Mr Jones wrote you last April and your wifes Brother but you must have left the valley and not received them. Aunt Sheratt as provided a sum of money for you and if you have not enough off money to bring you from New Orleans, and will write to Mr. Jones and tell him the sum that you want and how to direct it, it will be immediately sent. This was the purport of Mr. Jones letter which you have not received. Aunt Bayley is dead last March. She was only ill about 3 days. I have provided you a house it is one of my own at QuinaBrook and if you do not like the situation you can stay in it until you suit yourself better. I will keep it empty till you come home. William as let your old house to a yearly tenant and there is no chance of you having it again. We have corn very dear at 14/- and 15/- but we have had an exelant harvist and it is now little more than half the price. We will send you a newspaper every week and we hope you will write back as soon as you receive this stating wether you require any money sent or not. The money Aunt Sheratt as put aside for you will give you a good start, for she says being as your Father left you nothing she will make amend, but she says *that you shall not have it unless you come to England. Aunt Sherratt, Aunt Challinor, myself and wife, Mr Jones, Richard, Mary Ann, etc etc send their kind love to you and all wish to see you amongst them again soon.*

I remain,   My Dear Brother,

Your affectionate Brother, THOMAS HOLDING

At these times, before it was possible to 'wire' money across the Atlantic Ocean, it is thought possible that their voyage home was paid to a shipping company in Liverpool, which operated a regular run to and from New Orleans. We can only guess at the hardship that the family must have endured whilst they awaited the arrival of the ship to take them home.

Their homecoming to Prees must have been a joyous affair, but it is hard to believe Daniel's trials and tribulations had not left him a broken man. Three children had been born and three had died in North America. However, there is conflicting information as in his later life, Ephraim George said that his father wrote to one of his wife's relations saying: *how he* (Daniel) *regretted beyond expression, his return to England and hoped that the Lord would spare him in health so that he could return to Zion.* This statement, however, contrasts sharply with the fact that on 19 August 1855, just over a year after his homecoming, Thomas had all four of his children re-baptised at the local chapel in Whixall. Eleven months later, Sarah gave birth to their last child, Mary Ann Holding.

There is evidence that Daniel was very popular with locals in and around the village, but possibly any negative gossip in a small god-fearing community was never far from his side. How much this troubled him is impossible to say, but a little over two years after returning to Prees on 6 Aug 1856, at the young age of 44, he passed away. The cause of death was ulceration of the stomach and it would be surprising if his trials over the previous four years or so had not been a major contributor to his early demise.

At the time of their father's death, the ages of his children were Thomas Hiram 12, Sarah Jane 9, Ephraim George 7, Richard 3 and newly born Mary Ann. By this time Thomas Hiram was apprenticed to the local village tailor and we shall return to his remarkable life story later, but for the time being, we remain with Sarah and her other four children. Within a year or so she had established a relationship with Thomas Clayton who was employed as a Foreman Platelayer on the local railway line being built in the vicinity. Records show that her movements traced the building of the line and on 30 June 1859, she gave birth to a son, Thomas Clayton Holding, and three years later to a daughter, Maria Clayton Holding, but this, her last child, sadly passed on when she was just 15 months old. It seems that Sarah never lost sight of her Mormon beliefs and it would have been a proud day for her when in September 1867, Ephraim was ordained as a priest in the church at Chester.

On 12 July 1870, Ephraim loaded his belongings (a box, a carpet bag and a rug) on board the steamship *SS Manhattan* and two weeks later he disembarked in New York. From there, he proceeded by train via Pittsburg and Chicago to Omaha, where three days later, he '*washed in the Mississippi river*'. Four days later, less than one month after leaving Liverpool, he arrived in Ogden, Utah. This is in comparison to the eight-month trek of just 17 years earlier.

Within four years, Ephraim wired money to pay for the emigration of his 11-year-old brother, Thomas Clayton, and a few years later funded the emigration of his mother, Sarah. On 14 October 1875 she, her daughter Mary Ann (19), and adopted daughter, Elizabeth Ann Evans (7) boarded the SS *Dakota* and three weeks later they safely disembarked from the inaugural railway service into Salt Lake City. We can only guess at reasons why her second 'husband' Thomas Clayton did not accompany her on her second emigration – see later chapter. She had left behind three of her children who were now settled in the 'English' way of life. Thomas Hiram Holding the tailor and Sarah Darlington married in Shropshire in 1869, Sarah Jane Holding and Scotsman tailor, James Bryden, married in 1871 and four days after Sarah's departure for Salt Lake City in 1875 bootmaker and canvasser Richard Holding and Rosanna Smith were also married. During her lifetime, Sarah had given birth to 11 children, and of those, five had died at a young age. Thomas Hiram, Sarah Jane and Richard Holding lived out their lives in England, while the other three, Ephraim George, Mary Ann and Thomas Clayton Holding lived out their lives in the USA. Except for the odd visit, both sides remained an ocean apart, but were regular letter writers.

Sarah Holding, nee Middleton

Born in 1823 in Prees, Shropshire, England. Died in Salt Lake City, Utah, USA in 1912.

During Sarah's second westward Atlantic crossing, her daughter, Mary Ann, fell in love with Bedson Eardley, a returning missionary and captain of the company of emigrating 'Saints'. They were married in Salt Lake City on 8 May 1876. She was Bedson Eardley's second wife. Meanwhile, the last of Sarah's children, Thomas Clayton Holding, married twice in Salt Lake City. His first marriage was to Lovina Pollard on 12 April 1883 followed by Catherine Davis on 29 May 1897.

At the age of 90, Sarah Holding, who emigrated twice to Salt Lake City, died there on 16 December 1912. She had survived her husband Daniel by 55 years.

Sarah's second eldest son, Ephraim George Holding married Mary Jane Clifton (1871) and established one of the first electrical lighting shops in Salt Lake City. He installed lighting in The Mormon Temple and died in 1927 from injuries sustained after being hit by a tram in San Diego, California.

Ephraim George Holding

Born 1849 in Prees, Shropshire, England and died in Salt Lake City, USA in 1927.

Ephraim George Holding on top of the Mormon Temple in Salt Lake City. Note the lack of safety harness, or apparently even a ladder.

Thomas Hiram Holding – the man

Finally, we return to the later life of Thomas Hiram Holding, whose character was forged as he sailed across the Atlantic Ocean and camped on the plains and mountains of the USA. He left Shropshire in 1853 as an 8-year-old child and returned the following year as a young man, with a wealth of experience beyond his years. His is a true tale of 'rags to riches'. From a humble start in life, he rose to the very top of his profession. Simply educated, he excelled in both business and leisure. He never lost his love for adventure and the outdoor life, camping, cycling and canoeing. In short, he lived his life to the full.

Following the completion of his apprenticeship at George Shinglor's tailoring shop in Prees, Shropshire, Thomas Hiram Holding and local girl Sarah Darlington married in 1869. The 1871 Census shows 36-year-old Thomas Hiram Holding at home in Wigford, close to the town centre of Lincoln. A decade later at the time of the 1881 Census, they had relocated to Cheltenham in Gloucestershire where 36-year-old Thomas Hiram and 40-year-old Sarah reside with their four children, 10-year-old Edgar Thomas, Nelly 7, Frank 6 and Clement who is 5. The last three children were born in Banbury, Oxfordshire indicating that they resided there before moving to Cheltenham. Finally, by 1891 they had settled in Fulham, London where they lived for the remains of their lives.

At some time between 1871 and 1891, Thomas Hiram adopted, and possibly adapted, a system of measuring clients which produced neater fitting garments. This process may have been based upon a system known as, *'The Tailors' Transfer or, a New and Improved System of Measurement and Garment Cutting'* which had been patented by William R. Acton of Virginia', USA, as early as 1846. Both systems were complex, not easy to understand and therefore were best taught in a classroom setting. Holding's system grew rapidly in popularity and enabled Thomas Hiram and his family to reside in London where his business addresses were listed as 7 Maddox Street, Bond Street, Mayfair, London W1, and The London Cutting School at 3 Adelaide Street, Charing Cross, London. In his book *Uniforms of the British Army, Navy and Court*, published in 1894 he stated of the, *School of Cutting*. *'Several thousand pupils have passed our hands, and many hold posts at the greatest houses in England.'* In addition to making bespoke clothes for Army and Navy Officers, he also made fashionable clothes for the wealthy and his business was *by Royal Appointment*.

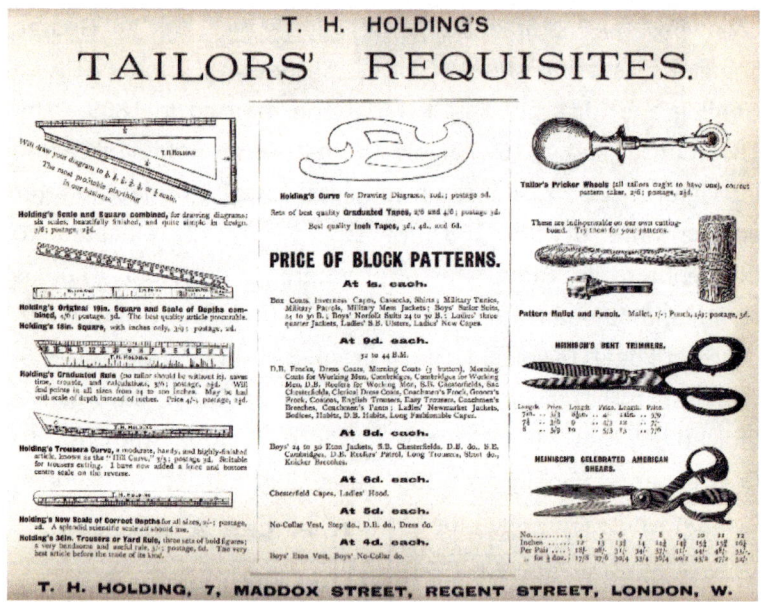

A full page advertisement copied from his book, Uniforms of the British Army, Navy, and Court.

In the left hand column, third from the top, can be seen an item called *Holding's Graduated Rule and on* 13 July 1882 *Tailor and Cutter* magazine wrote, 'Mr Holding having sent us a new graduated rule for our inspection and being desirous of that we should notice it.'

For many years he was the editor of *Tailor and Cutter* and *London Tailor* magazines and he also served as a London magistrate, riding to court on his bicycle.

In a clear sign that he remained in close touch with his siblings in Utah, he named their residence at 6 Fulham Park Gardens, Fulham, as '*Hazel Dean*' in memory of Thomas Clayton Holding's child, who died in Salt Lake City in 1903. The name '*Hazel Dean*' was neatly hand painted on the lintel forming an arch over the front porch.

The front porch of their home in Fulham, London.

Thomas Hiram Holding wrote over 20 books, many of which remain in print to this day. Their titles include:
The Camper's Handbook,
Watery Wanderings 'mid Western Lochs,
The Cruise of the Osprey,
Cycle and Camp,
Uniforms of the British Army, Navy and Court,
Late Victorian Women's Tailoring,
British Liveries,
Ladies Cutting Made Easy and *Coats; How to Cut Them,*
Coat Cutting,
Trousers, Vest, Breeches and Gaiter Cutting,
Cutting for Stout Men,
Ladies Garment Cutting,
British Livery Cutting.

Thought to be an early photograph.

Thomas Hiram Holding's book, **Ladies Garment Cutting**, first published in 1890, showed that he was not above flattery and includes the following dedication –

TO THE LADY ... Who nature has cast in a graceful mould, Who's taste is quiet and her style refined, Whose patience with her Tailor equals the charm of an amiable manner, Whose sense of self respect teaches her how to dress like the lady she is, But whose good sense saves her from extravagance, Who, while not regardless of anything that may become her station in matters of dress, Yet does not make it the aim of her life. THIS BOOK, Written to help in ministering to her tastes, IS, WITH ALL DEFERENCE, RESPECTFULLY DEDICATED BY THE AUTHOR.

Extract from Late Victorian Women's Tailoring

Extracts from Late Victorian Women's Tailoring

By the turn of the nineteenth century the Women's Rights Movement was gathering pace; many women were no longer content with a life constrained within the family home. They took up pursuits such as hiking, climbing and cycling where long skirts were impractical. Recognising a need in 1901 Thomas applied for and was granted a patent title: *Knickerbocker, Breeches and Like Garments.*

Lady cyclist wearing Knickerbockers of the type patented by Thomas Hiram Holding in 1902.

In the following year of 1902 he applied for a second patent: *Improvements in and relating to driving aprons* which recognised the need for waterproof capes and aprons to wear in roofless automobiles. Two years later there was a third patent: *Improved Waterproof Garment.* It is thought that at least some of these motoring-related items may have been coated with impervious rubber.

Encyclopaedia Britannica credits him as follows – *The founder of modern recreational camping was Thomas Hiram Holding who wrote the first camper's handbook in 1908.*

In his book **Cycle and Camp**, first published in 1898 he relates how he and his friends cycle, camp and canoe around Connemara, Ireland.

At the start of Chapter 1, he declares his unquestionable love of camping.

'Who can question them? Only those who have never tried camping. All the horrors which outsiders fear and which they threaten us we neither meet nor find. In fact they don't exist. Camping is nearly always delightful, for a holiday at least, and if well managed is pleasant and healthy, as well as cheap, for a more protracted period. But it is not a lazy life – far from it. The question comes in here, perhaps, as to which holiday is the most beneficial – LOAFING or ACTIVITY? He who would spend a holiday in shear laziness should take luxurious lodgings or quarter himself at a splendid hotel, and next to the strain and exertion of eating, do literally, nothing. To most men, however, young or middle aged, who lead active lives and who are gifted with average energy, something less dormant is, surely, an advantage. The camp affords this:- Exercise without fatigue; fresh air at night and day, and sufficient excitement to create interest.'

In Chapter XIII he provides design details for a tent of suitable dimensions for cycling and camping made from linen. A later design was said to have been manufactured from silk and weighed only 11 ounces (0.3 kg), and small enough to fit into his pocket. The ridge pole doubled as his fishing rod.

In his recreational time, he founded *The Association of Cycle Campers* which merged with other clubs to evolve into *The Camping and Caravanning Club of Great Britain* whose membership today exceeds 700,000.

Photographs copied from his book, Cycle and Camp

CYCLE CAMPING—A FICTION.

Or the above might be titled – How not to do it?

"FIVE O'CLOCK TEA."

It is difficult to believe that Thomas Hiram Holding's book **Uniforms of the British Army, Navy, and Court** did not influence designs of the album cover for the Beatles Sergeant Pepper.

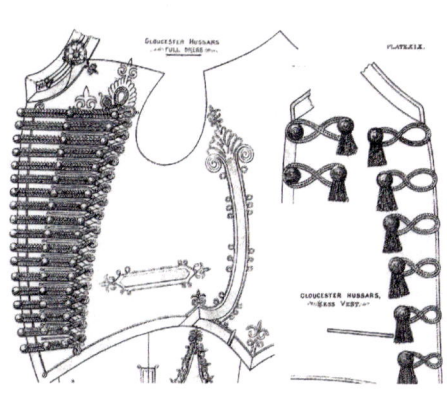

Jacket design for the Gloucester Hussars by Thomas Hiram Holding

Book cover of Uniforms of the British Army, Navy and Court, first published in May 1894.

Uniform examples from left to right, The King's Royal Rifles, Scottish Rifles,, Royal Scots Greys and the Gordon Highlanders.

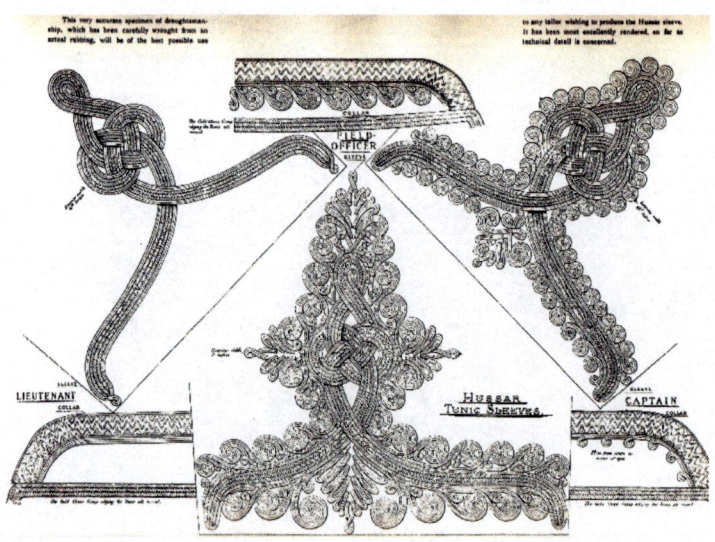

Some examples of intricate embroidery shown in the book.

Thomas and Sarah had five children, Edgar Thomas, Nelly, Frank and Clement. The name of the fifth child is unknown and may have died young. Edgar Thomas Holding became a renowned watercolour artist and became Secretary to the Royal Watercolour Society at the same time that Sir Russell Flint was the president.

Thomas Hiram Holding's death was recorded in London in 1930 having survived his wife Sarah by 5 years.

Finally, we return to Thomas Hiram's letter referred to previously and written in 1928 just two years before his death. As we have seen throughout this chronicle it is personal memories that bring it to life and Thomas' letter is no exception. Here he is replying to a letter from his nephew Clifford Richard Holding who he mistakenly refers to as his grandson.

6, Fulham Park Gardens, London SW6

Dear Grandson, *Dated 1928*

I am most pleased to try to give you the information – in brief – which I believe NO other person now living can know anything of the very query you have made. I congratulate you on so laudible an effort. I am sorry I have no typewriter expert at my hand just now. You mey ken I have dictated <u>all the books</u> I have written and hundreds of articles in all "sorts and sizes" of events in my life.

My wicked old grandfather (Richard) was born I believe at Steele Heath, Salop 140 years or so ago. He was a Tailor & married a rich woman from Belvideer (beyond Whitchurch). She owned much property in Whitchurch Salop, and round about

Steel also, but he was a coarse man, and to me, as a lad, said nasty things in my presence to others.

My father was Daniel Holding a son of the old one. He was a much respected man of fiery temper soon over. We lived at Coton on High Way between Chester and salop. Now I have touched on a delicate point indeed. The old man had a younger sister who unfortunately had at Market Drayton a "chance child" as they put it in these days. He it was when grown up able to carry on the tailoring - which was being done at the house of the farmers - ie what they still call in tailor's language <u>Whipping the Cat!</u>

Grandfather (Richard) *made a Will, for round the Heath there are several properties one of which he Willed* <u>TO ME</u> *- a snug black and white house to be mine, and my father had also been Willed in the same way. When the end ie separation was about to be he had, unknown to father he cut out his portion save £5 only and said "serve him right to go gallivanting about to Horse Ponds with so called Saints". Every horse pond was soon in use for baptising Mormon converts. I saw it as a new church. I walked miles to see the baptisms in Horse ponds, etc.Very soon after we emigrated he* (grandfather Richard) *died. In the fine old Churchyard on top of the lofty Roman Way of Prees he was buried in a big stone Vault* <u>to left</u> *of Church his name can still be seen.*

He (father Daniel) *was carried to Prees churchyard 3.5 miles on men's shoulders and I saw the shallow grave of deal boards buried. NB There is a big vault in the Prees grave yard – which by the way 300 feet above the village. Instead of them opening the vault which had but three bodies in it Himself his wife and Mrs Shirrat I think it.*

More than once I have tried to find the Mound ie grave but alas theres hundreds buried there and Poor Daniel Holding the tailor cant be found.

All this of course follows our crossing of the Prairies fifteen hundred miles out to salt Lake City three years after the Mormons under Brigham Young created what is now a vast City of Sky-scrapers.

End of letter.

Today, it is a simple matter to visit that same churchyard and imagine, a hundred years or so ago, one of Thomas Hiram Holding's visits. Perhaps he pitched his lightweight tent in a nearby pasture, perhaps he rested his bicycle against the wall under the ancient yew tree.

Without a doubt, he would have paused to read again the inscription dedicated to his grandfather on the old family tomb,

'In memory of Richard Houlding of Steele ....

Around the rear of the church, he would have walked the rows, pausing to check the inscriptions. We recall his words:

..... 'More than once I have tried to find the Mound ie grave but alas theres hundreds buried there and poor Daniel Holding the tailor cant be found.'

Afterword

As we noted at the beginning of this book, we were very fortunate to have found so much documentary evidence to support our ancestor's extraordinary lives, however, some questions perhaps remain. The reader might, for instance, wonder why Sarah Holding's second 'husband' Thomas Clayton did not accompany her when she returned to Salt Lake City in 1875. It is hard to be absolutely certain but the following explanation fits what few facts we have. Firstly, despite it being a legal requirement at that time, no record of a marriage registration has been found between them. Secondly, when Sarah registered the birth of her last two children, Thomas Clayton Holding and Maria Clayton Holding, the father's name was not listed on the birth certificate. At that time this was not permitted unless the father was present at the registration. However, after the death of 15-month-old Maria, the father was named on the death certificate as Thomas Clayton. The death was recorded by Maria's step-sister Sarah Jane Holding, who stated that she was present at the time of death. Thirdly, Thomas Clayton's occupation was given as a Foreman Railway Platelayer, in other words, he led a team that laid railway tracks and at about the time of the death of Sarah's first husband Daniel, the railway was being constructed through the village Prees. The following is one explanation which fits these facts, but it must be stressed that there may be others.

It seems likely, that following the death of her husband, Sarah Holding and Thomas Clayton formed a symbiotic relationship; in short, they both needed each other. Since the Latter Day Saints did not welcome the idea of single women travelling to Salt Lake City and thereby consuming precious resources, Sarah would have needed Thomas's skills to support an application for a second assisted passage. For his part, Thomas needed a woman to 'keep house', which often meant living in tented villages, which were moved in a nomadic style alongside the tracks. Sarah's experiences, coping with cold and wet conditions, mud, tents, campfires, etc. on the Mormon Trail would have served her well. There can be little doubt that women with those skills would have been few and far between.

Away from civilisation, prying eyes and gossip, families often wrote their own rule book. A marriage in the traditional sense was often impractical and it was quite common for a couple to marry, by 'stepping over the brush'. Since this was not a formal marriage then there was no requirement for it to be officially registered, but in the eyes of those present, you were considered to be husband and wife. It was said that the men lived on bread and beer, with meat on special occasions. The meat would typically be boiled in a pot over an open campfire, with the meat suspended on a piece of string. Whilst the men ate the meat, the rest of the family shared the broth, with perhaps a cob of bread to soak it up. Eventually, the family may have passed through a town or village where it would have been possible for the mother to formally register any births, and if the father was unable to attend, then this might account for why his name did not appear on either of the certificates.

As we have witnessed, only six of Sarah Holding's eleven children survived through to adulthood, three died in England, and the other three in Utah, USA. Of the three who died in England, Sarah Jane's death is recorded in Birmingham in 1925, the same location as Richard who followed her in 1934, and as we have already recorded the eldest child Thomas Hiram died in Fulham, London in 1930. Meanwhile, across 'the pond', Ephraim George died in 1927 in Salt Lake City, the same location as Thomas Clayton in 1932 and Mary Ann in 1940. It has been said that as he was dying Thomas Clayton was trying to say something to the family. Perhaps he wanted to say that his birth had been illegitimate, a fact that according to the Mormon religion would have excluded him from the Kingdom of Heaven. It is sad to think that he may have lived under this shadow for his whole life.

However, we do not want to end this book on a dark note, and so we will finish with a rather cheeky and amusing snap-shot into Sarah Jane's life written by Clifford Richard Holding. It was Clifford who had written to Thomas Hiram Holding in 1928 to enquire about their family's history. And it was Sarah Jane whose head was crushed under the wagon wheel. In 1963 Clifford wrote the following.

Beyond the paper shop was the tailor's shop kept by James Bryden. His wife was my grandfather's sister and the whole family went to Chapel with us, first to Ruskin Hall and later to Beaumont Road, and the various daughters taught in the Sunday school. There seemed to be a great number of these and a boy, too, who suffered constantly from boils and could usually be seen with a piece of celluloid over one cheek, held in position by elastic passed around his head (presumably he is referring to himself). *The several daughters like their mother, were almost mouse-like, creatures always busy about the house it seemed to me. James Richard Bryden himself was a more robust character – 'stiff' they would have called him in the north – and his style of tailoring was a 'lap behind' the current fashion. I can well remember the sort of criticisms which used to be levied about 'cut' and the buttons in unexpected places. The work was so good and the stuff so tough that the clothes were passed down the family with increasing despair. My uncle Sydney Snead worked for James Bryden, sitting downstairs in the shop in the workroom, which could also be reached by a back door at ground level owing to the steep slope of the land. Here we could discover him sitting patiently, hand stitching or pressing with the sizzling iron reeking the pungent smell of singed soap. It was in the shop above that mother used to buy our Eton collars, shirts, underwear and even the occasional tie, but the whole commerce seemed more of a duty than a pleasure for all concerned.*

Acknowledgements

Firstly, many thanks to Aunt Kath, little did she realise what she had started. Also thanks to Clifford Richard Holding who as a young man wrote to Thomas Hiram Holding in 1928 and valued the reply so highly that he retained it into his later years.

This work would not be complete without acknowledging the evocative images created by Frederick Hawkins Piercy, whose engravings and woodcuts have been used to illustrate this work. His journey was made when he was just twenty three and his book, Route from Liverpool to Great Salt Lake Valley, first published in 1855 with facsimile copies in recent years.

Frederick Hawkins Piercy (1830 – 1891) and his book

Thanks are given to members of the writer's family for their assistance with editing – Darryl, Margaret, Carolyn and Judith – and also to Jackie Tee for illustrating the map, and Valeria Leonova for the book cover.

Contacts

Compilation and text by Carl White
sploshandpop@gmail.com

Map Illustration by Jacqueline Tee
www.wonkymouse.com

Book cover by Valeria Leonova
www.facebook.com/artvaleriaillustrator/

Thomas Hiram Holding, reprinted from his book
Uniforms of the British Army, Navy and Court.

Printed in Dunstable, United Kingdom

6733484OR00047